The World of Sharks

Get to Know the Fascinating
Creatures of the Oceans

LITTLE
GESTALTEN

Shark Species

Great White Shark
pp. 24–25

Shortfin Mako Shark
pp. 26–27

Great Hammerhead Shark
pp. 36–37

Whale Shark
pp. 18–20

Longnose Saw Shark
pp. 38–39

Basking Shark
pp. 42–43

Shark Species

Zebra Shark
pp. 44–45

Spotted Wobbegong Shark
pp. 50–51

Bull Shark
pp. 52–53

Frilled Shark
p. 57

Goblin Shark
p. 56

Tiger Shark
pp. 58–59

Angel Shark
pp. 60–61

Other Topics

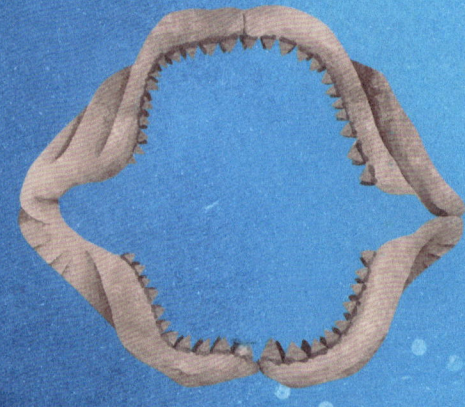

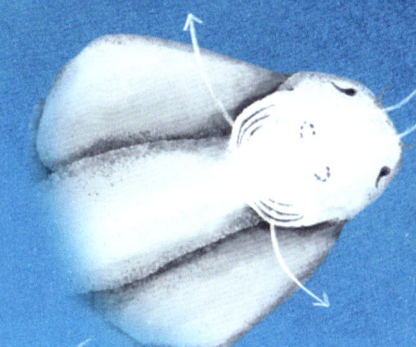

Finned and Fascinating

Sharks have lived on Earth since before the time of the dinosaurs. They are found in every ocean and even in some rivers. Some are huge, while others are small. Some are fierce, some are gentle and curious, and some are timid. Some travel the world, and some stay close to home. But wherever they are and however they live, sharks play a very important role in keeping the oceans healthy and full of life.

In this book, you will meet just a few of the many kinds of sharks alive today. You will learn a little about their finely tuned senses and amazing abilities. You will also see that there is much we still do not know about them. Researchers who study sharks are finding out new things every day. But one thing we know for sure is that the world of sharks is a fascinating place. Enjoy your visit here!

What Is a Shark?

Sharks are fish—but not just any fish. Instead of bones, sharks have skeletons made of cartilage. Cartilage is the strong, bendy stuff found in your ears and the tip of your nose. Cartilage is lighter and more flexible than bone. This help helps make sharks fast and agile.

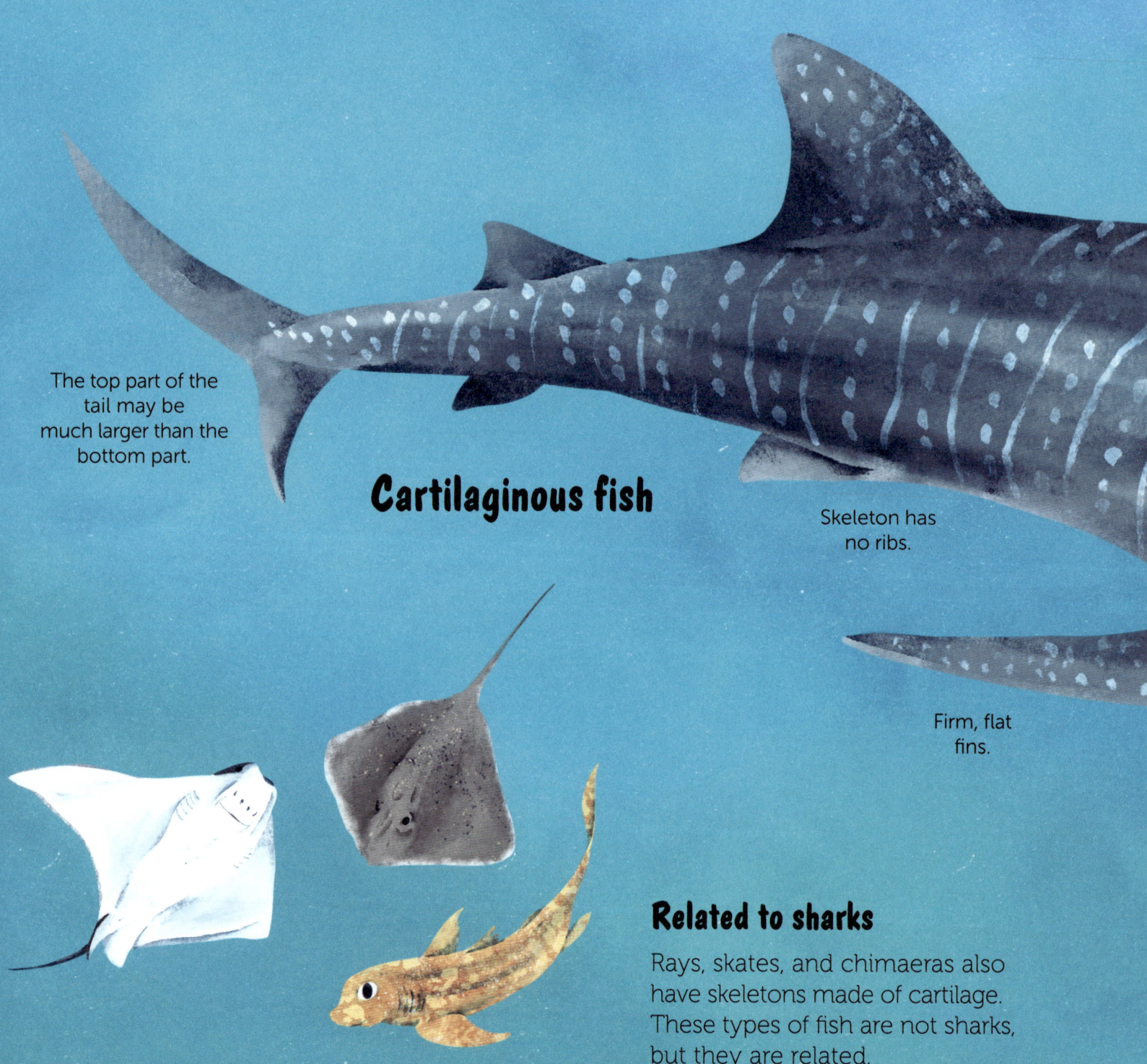

The top part of the tail may be much larger than the bottom part.

Cartilaginous fish

Skeleton has no ribs.

Firm, flat fins.

Related to sharks

Rays, skates, and chimaeras also have skeletons made of cartilage. These types of fish are not sharks, but they are related.

Bony fish

Flexible, ridged fins.

Gills are covered.

Nostrils on the upper side of the head.

The top and bottom of their tail are usually the same shape and size.

Mouth at the front tip of the head.

Skeleton has ribs.

Flat, rounded scales.

Tough, ridged skin.

Exposed gills.

Mouth on the underside of the head.

Nostrils on the underside of the head.

The Body of a Shark

Sharks come in many shapes and sizes. One kind of shark can look very different from another. All sharks have skeletons made of cartilage, but not all fish with cartilage skeletons are sharks. So what makes a shark a shark?

There are many different sharks in this book, and the body parts shown in this picture are common to all sharks.

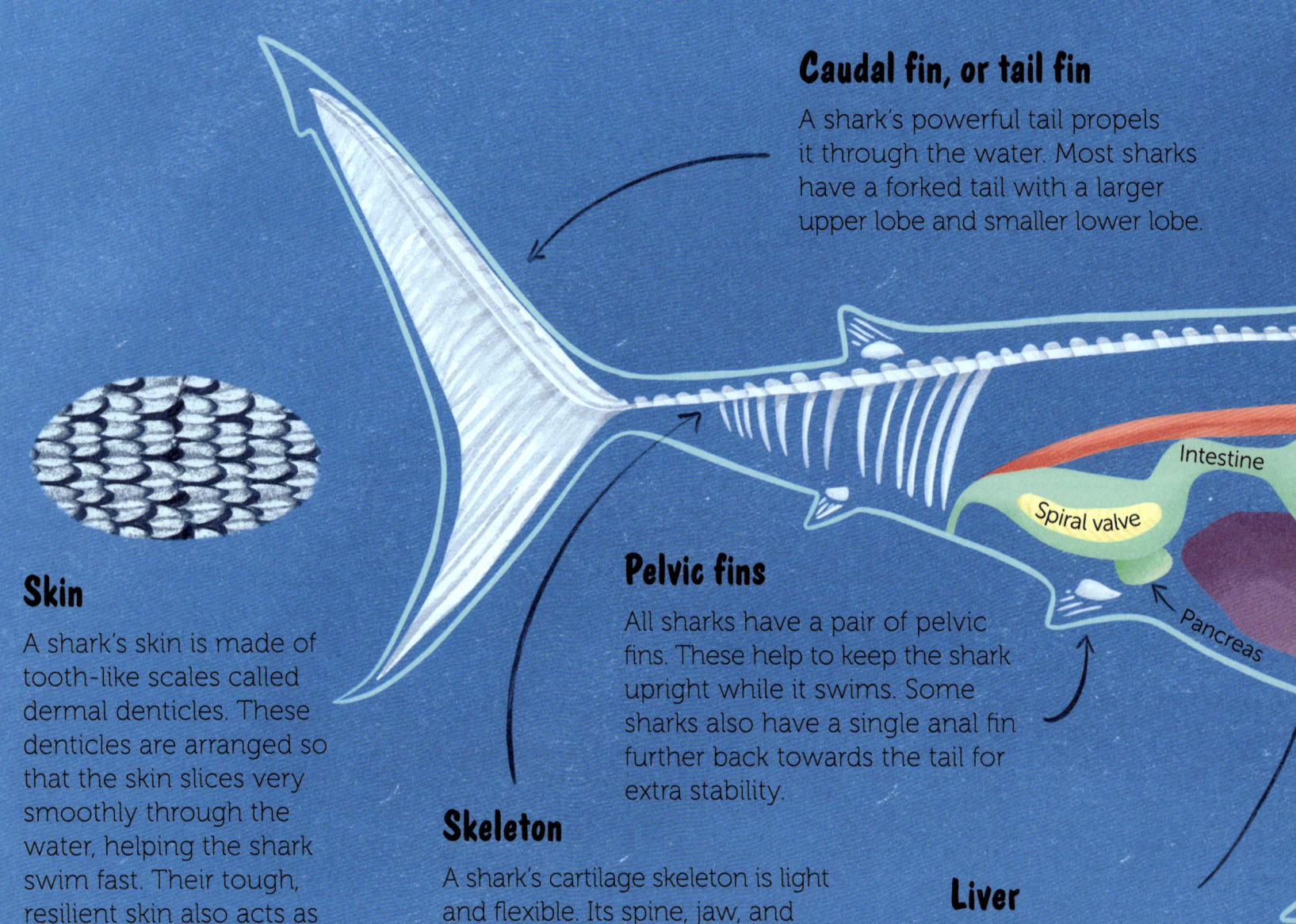

Caudal fin, or tail fin

A shark's powerful tail propels it through the water. Most sharks have a forked tail with a larger upper lobe and smaller lower lobe.

Intestine

Spiral valve

Pancreas

Skin

A shark's skin is made of tooth-like scales called dermal denticles. These denticles are arranged so that the skin slices very smoothly through the water, helping the shark swim fast. Their tough, resilient skin also acts as a flexible form of armor.

Pelvic fins

All sharks have a pair of pelvic fins. These help to keep the shark upright while it swims. Some sharks also have a single anal fin further back towards the tail for extra stability.

Skeleton

A shark's cartilage skeleton is light and flexible. Its spine, jaw, and skull are reinforced with extra minerals that make these body parts stronger and more rigid.

Liver

A shark's large liver is full of oils that help the shark to stay buoyant, or floating, in the water.

Dorsal fin

All sharks have at least one dorsal fin, and some have two. The dorsal fin helps the shark to stay upright while it swims. Some sharks have a sharp spine as part of their dorsal fins.

Did you know?

Total length: the length of a shark from the tip of its snout to the furthest tip of its tail. "Total length" can be used to compare the size of two sharks of the same type.

Fork length: the length of a shark from the tip of its snout to the nearest point in the fork of its tail. Using "fork length" makes it easier to compare the size of different types of sharks with different tail shapes.

Dorsal side: the back of a shark

olfactory bulb

Brain

Kidney

Stomach

Heart

Ventral side: the belly of a shark

Pectoral fins

A shark's pectoral fins are the front fins that it has on each side. These help the shark steer through the water by doing turns, lifts, and dives.

Gills

Sharks do not breathe air, but they still need oxygen. Their gills take in oxygen from the water as they flow through it. Most sharks have five gills on each side.

Teeth

Shark teeth are arranged in several rows, one behind the other. When one tooth falls out, the tooth behind it moves forward to fill the empty space. A shark may lose and replace thousands of teeth over its life.

The Evolution of Sharks

Imagine the Earth more than 450 million years ago. On the barren, rocky land, some tiny plants are just beginning to grow. There are no trees or bushes, no ferns, flowers, or grasses, and no animals. Even the dinosaurs will not appear for another 100 million years.

But the seas are teeming with life. Small ocean creatures are starting to appear. One family of fish has split off from the others and is beginning to evolve a skeleton made of cartilage instead of bone. These fish are the ancestors of all the sharks that have ever been.

By about 350 million years ago, many different kinds of shark lived in oceans all around the world.

About 450 million years ago   400   350   300   250

The early bony fish keep evolving, becoming the ancestors of other fish. These are also the ancestors of all other animals with a bony skeleton, including reptiles, birds, and mammals such as you.

This early ancestor of sharks had no teeth and was probably not much longer than one of your fingers.

About 420 million years ago, one family of cartilaginous fish split off from the others. These evolved into skates, rays, and chimaera.

About 250 million years ago, many fish and other ocean creatures died out. Of all the different kinds of shark, only a few survived. These became the ancestors of the sharks that live today.

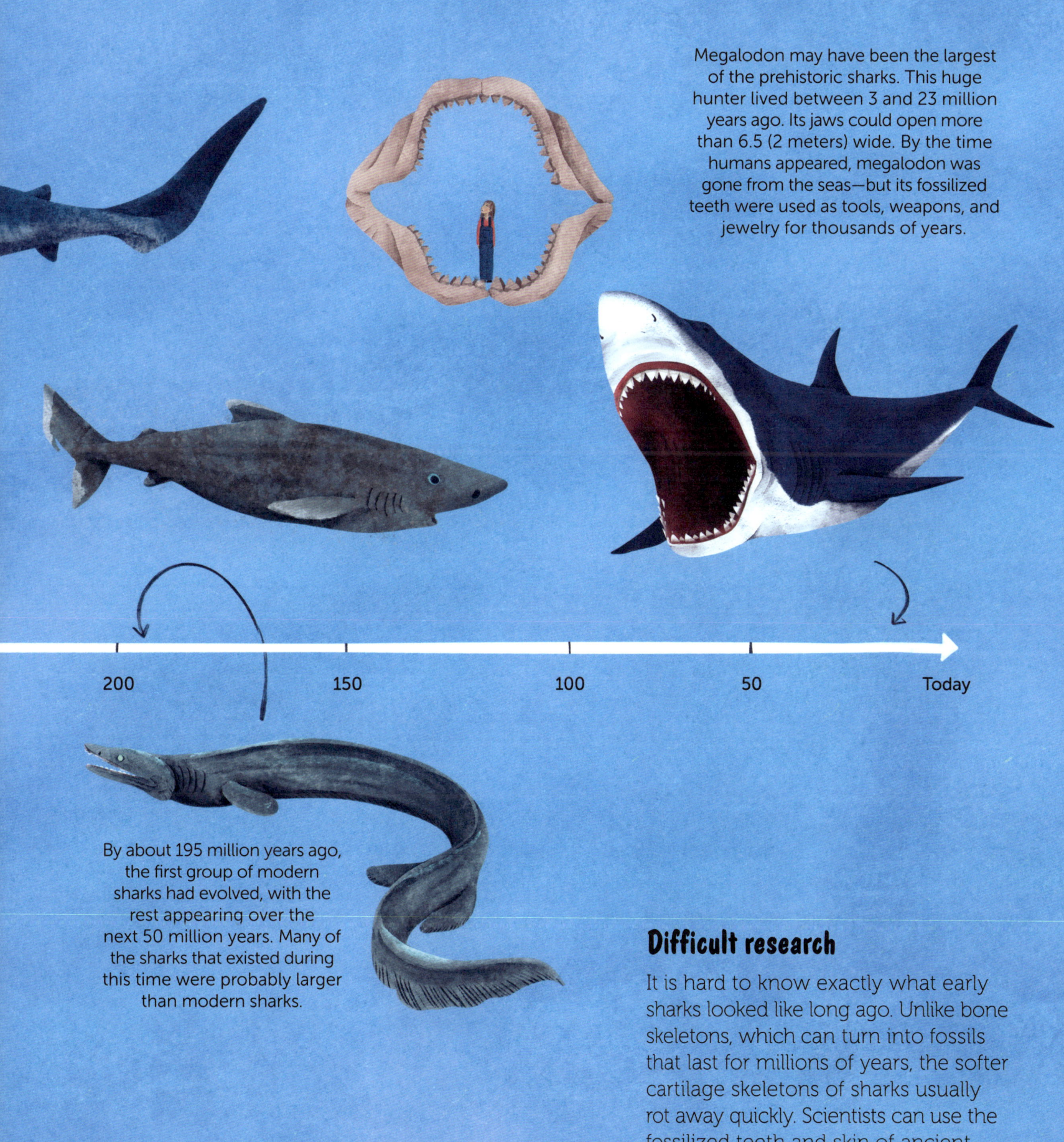

Megalodon may have been the largest of the prehistoric sharks. This huge hunter lived between 3 and 23 million years ago. Its jaws could open more than 6.5 (2 meters) wide. By the time humans appeared, megalodon was gone from the seas—but its fossilized teeth were used as tools, weapons, and jewelry for thousands of years.

200   150   100   50   Today

By about 195 million years ago, the first group of modern sharks had evolved, with the rest appearing over the next 50 million years. Many of the sharks that existed during this time were probably larger than modern sharks.

Difficult research

It is hard to know exactly what early sharks looked like long ago. Unlike bone skeletons, which can turn into fossils that last for millions of years, the softer cartilage skeletons of sharks usually rot away quickly. Scientists can use the fossilized teeth and skin of ancient sharks to help piece together the puzzle of how sharks came to be.

Sharks Today

Scientists organize the sharks that exist today into eight main groups. Some of these groups contain many different kinds of shark, while others have only a few. You can see some examples of the sharks in each group here.

Did you know?
The bull shark does not belong to the bullhead group of sharks. A bull shark is a kind of ground shark (see page 52).

Sixgill sharks

Sixgill sharks may be the most ancient type of shark alive today. Sharks in this group have six or seven pairs of gill slits, and only one dorsal fin. They often live in the very deep sea.

Ground sharks

Ground sharks make up the biggest group of sharks in the world today. This group includes the hammerhead shark and blue shark. Ground sharks have a see-through eyelid that helps protect the eye.

Carpet Sharks

Many kinds of carpet shark are found mostly near the ocean floor in shallow seas. Most have colorful markings. Their mouths are at the very front of their snouts.

Mackerel sharks

The mackerel shark group includes some of the best-known sharks, including the great white shark and the shortfin mako shark. Their mouths are on the underside of their snouts, extending past the eye.

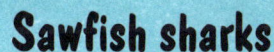

Sawfish sharks

Sawfish sharks are easy to identify by their long toothy snouts. Some saw shark species have six pairs of gill slits, while others have five.

Dogfish sharks

There are more than 100 kinds of dogfish shark. These sharks have two dorsal fins and no anal fin. Some dogfish sharks have a sharp, poisonous spine on one or both dorsal fins.

Angel sharks

Angel sharks have broad, flat bodies with coloring that helps them blend into the ocean floor. They have two dorsal fins and no anal fin.

Bullhead sharks

Most kinds of bullhead sharks are quite small. They have two dorsal fins, each with a sturdy spike. They get their name from the horn-like bumps on their heads.

Whale Shark

The whale shark is easy to identify because of its wide, flat head, the "checkerboard" pattern of white dots and lines on its dark blue-gray or brown-gray skin … and its size. It is the largest of all sharks, and the biggest fish in the world. An adult whale shark can be longer than a school bus, but there is nothing to fear: this polka-dotted carpet shark is a gentle giant.

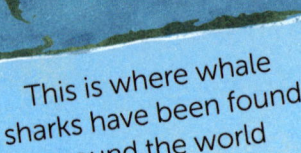

This is where whale sharks have been found around the world

Filter feeding

The whale shark lives in the warm waters of tropical oceans around the world. It feeds on creatures such as small plants, fish, and squid. It swims along slowly with its mouth open or hangs tail-down in the water and opens and closes its mouth to gulp in mouthfuls of water filled with its prey. The whale shark swallows its prey while the water flows back out through its gills. This is called filter feeding, and you can read more about it on page 41.

Small food for big fish

Because its food is very small, the whale shark must eat a lot of it. It spends over eight hours feeding every day, and travels thousands of miles each year following its food around the oceans.

Researchers believe that whale sharks can live from 60 to 100 years. A whale shark that lives to be 100 will have filtered almost 400 million gallons (1.5 billion liters) of seawater in its lifetime.

The arrangement of spots and stripes on a whale shark's body blends into the pattern of light sparkling on the water's surface, making it harder to spot from above.

A whale shark's skin can be more than 4 inches (10 centimeters) thick.

Whale sharks have a layer of dermal denticles covering their eyeballs. This helps protect their eyes from being scratched. Whale sharks can also pull their eyeballs deep into their heads.

Several hard ridges, or keels, extend along the whale shark's body. These ridges help it glide more smoothly through the water.

A whale shark's mouth, filters, and gills make up almost one third of its total body length.

A whale shark's jaws can open more than 5 feet (1.5 meters) wide. Even though they are filter feeders, whale sharks have more than 300 rows of tiny teeth.

Length: 40 feet (12 meters)
Mass: 15 tons (14 tonnes)

Seven Senses

Sharks are busy creatures. They catch food, find safe places to shelter in and rest, and choose companions to spend time with. They also have to stay alert for danger. Some sharks travel long distances, often in the complete darkness of the deep ocean.

Humans experience the world using a combination of our five different senses: sight, smell, hearing, touch, and taste. Sharks use all of these senses too, plus at least two more that are particularly helpful in the dark.

Sensing moving water

Like all fish, sharks have a lateral line organ—a system of tubes with tiny openings— that helps them detect nearby movement in the water. It wraps around the head, along both sides of the body, and into the tail. A shark using its lateral line sensors can track the speed and direction of a single small fish darting by.

Touching

Although shark skin is very tough, it is still very sensitive. Sharks can use their sense of touch to feel their way along the sea floor or through narrow passageways in the dark. Some types of shark, such as the nurse shark, have whisker-like sensory organs called barbels on their snouts, which help them find prey hiding beneath sand or mud.

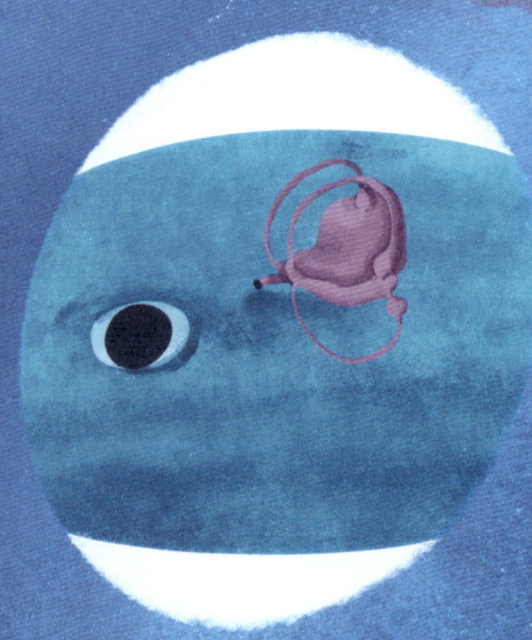

Hearing

A shark's ears are just small holes in its head, but they play a big role. Sharks have very good hearing that helps them detect food, company, or danger from miles away. Many sharks are particularly attuned to picking up thumping sounds that sound like injured prey.

Smelling

Scents travel a long way under water, but they become fainter as they mix with seawater. A shark can detect a single drop of fish blood in more than 13 gallons (50 liters) of sea water, and then track the scent to its source from hundreds of feet away.

When a shark swims, water flows in one nostril and out the other. This means the shark can keep smelling steadily as it tracks a scent through the water.

Seeing

Light does not travel well under water, so sharks cannot see very far—usually up to 30 or 65 feet (10 or 20 meters) away. Like cats, however, sharks are very good at seeing in dim light. The back of a shark's eyeball acts as a reflector that helps gather light within the eye. This can make shark eyes seem to glow green in the dark.

Some sharks are able to adjust their vision very quickly in changing light conditions, while others need more than an hour for their eyes to adjust.

Sensing electricity and magnetism

All living things give off tiny amounts of electricity—but only a few can sense it. Sharks have special sense organs called ampullae of Lorenzini that detect electric currents. Like lateral line organs, the ampullae are made up of openings that connect to a system of tubes under the shark's skin. The ampullae look like tiny dots on a shark's head, and can also sense the Earth's magnetic field. This may help some sharks migrate long distances without losing their way.

Tasting

A shark's sense of taste does not help it hunt, but it can help the shark decide what to eat. Different types of sharks have different favorite foods, and a shark may take a "test bite" to decide if the prey it has caught is good to eat. Most of a shark's taste sensors are in its gums, just behind its teeth.

Great White Shark

The great white shark is the largest of the mackerel sharks. Once fully grown, it is one of the sea's top predators. It migrates thousands of miles each year, hunting seals and sea lions as well as dolphins, porpoises, sea turtles, and even small whales. Its torpedo-shaped body can shoot through the water at speeds up to 30 miles per hour (50 kilometers per hour).

Did you know?
After a big meal, a great white may swim for more than a month before it eats again.

Skillful hunter

Great whites can see well both above and under water. This shark sometimes lifts its head above the waves to take a look around. This is called spy-hopping. After it has spotted its prey, the shark dives beneath the surface to attack from below.

The only sea animal known to hunt adult great whites is the orca.

Respect for the great white shark

In books and movies, this skilled hunter has been unfairly labelled a "man-eater." In reality, great whites do not hunt people on purpose. A few people are bitten by great whites each year. Scientists believe that these attacks probably happen because to a shark, a person swimming can look like an injured seal. With this shark's strong jaws and sharp, jagged teeth, even a test bite can do great damage. So it is still worthy of respect, even if it does not deserve its killer reputation.

This is where great white sharks have been found around the world

When this shark is attacking, its eyeballs roll right back into its skull. This protects them from being damaged.

At any given time, a great white has about 300 teeth in its mouth. It might grow and lose as many as 50,000 teeth in its lifetime.

The great white gets its name from its white belly.

Length: 16 feet (5 meters)
Mass: 1.3 tons (1.2 tonnes)

Shortfin Mako Shark

The shortfin mako shark is a sprinter among sharks. This mackerel shark can reach speeds of over 44 miles per hour (70 kilometers per hour) over short distances. It can also breach, or leap right out of the water, to heights of almost 20 feet (6 meters).

Like other mackerel sharks, the shortfin mako is partly warm-blooded. Its body temperature is a little higher than the surrounding water. This gives it the extra energy it needs for its bursts of speed and power.

The shortfin mako is also dressed for speed, with skin that has special flexible scales to help slice through the water.

The shortfin mako has a thick, muscular tail.

Did you know?
The name "mako" comes from the Māori word *makō*, which means "shark" or "shark's tooth."

A fast hunter

The shortfin mako is found in the open ocean all around the world. It hunts fast-swimming fish such as tuna and swordfish, as well as dolphins, porpoises, and smaller sharks.

This is where shortfin mako sharks have been found around the world

Shortfin makos are sometimes called blue pointers, because they have very pointed snouts.

Length: 13 feet (4 meters)
Mass: 1,100 pounds (500 kilograms)

The shortfin mako lives most of its life in the high seas, but comes close to shore to give birth. The pups are over 1.6 feet (50 centimeters) long when they are born. They spend their first years in coastal waters.

Sharks by the Shore

Rivers and streams pour into the sea along shorelines all around the world, carrying food and nutrients such as plants, minerals, and fish. At the same time, ocean currents push up against the land, bringing food up from the sea. In the bright, warm waters of shallow coastal areas, these rich waters serve up food for all kinds of living things, such as: meadows of sea grass and forests of kelp; shellfish and jellyfish; turtles and oysters and scuttling crabs; sea horses and sea slugs and sea stars; and fish of all shapes and colors. And through it all, hundreds of different species of shark are on the prowl.

The grey reef shark

Several different species of reef shark are found near coral reefs and lagoons in tropical seas. These grey reef sharks are speedy swimmers that gather in large groups to cruise the reefs by day—but at night they go their separate ways to hunt.

The sandbar shark

This shark cruises over sandy or muddy sea floors in shallow waters, searching for crabs, shrimp, squid, and fish to eat. These sharks have a brownish-grey body and are sometimes known as brown sharks.

The pyjama shark

This species lives near the coasts of southern Africa. It prefers rocky areas that have caves to hide in. This smaller ground shark eats small fish—including other small sharks—as well as squid and octopus.

Sharks in Rivers

In the hundreds of millions of years that sharks have existed, they have come to live in every part of the ocean. There are sharks to be found in rivers and lakes too. Some of these may be ocean sharks on the hunt for freshwater prey. Bull sharks, for example, will travel hundreds of miles upriver for food. Only a few types of shark spend most or all of their lives in fresh water.

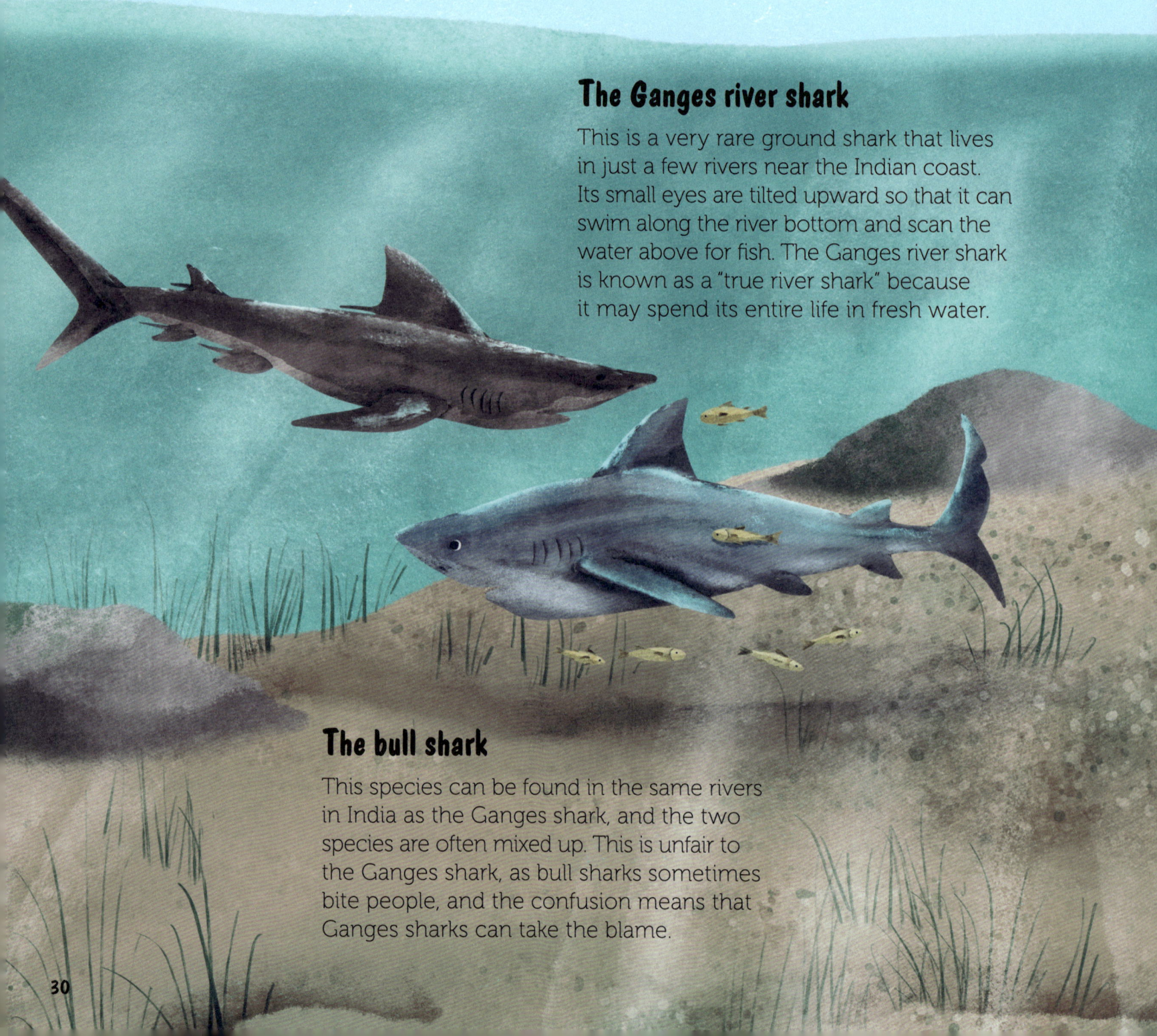

The Ganges river shark

This is a very rare ground shark that lives in just a few rivers near the Indian coast. Its small eyes are tilted upward so that it can swim along the river bottom and scan the water above for fish. The Ganges river shark is known as a "true river shark" because it may spend its entire life in fresh water.

The bull shark

This species can be found in the same rivers in India as the Ganges shark, and the two species are often mixed up. This is unfair to the Ganges shark, as bull sharks sometimes bite people, and the confusion means that Ganges sharks can take the blame.

River sharks

The speartooth shark and its relative the northern river shark live in the rivers and coastal waters of northern Australia and Papua New Guinea. As soon as the tide comes in, these sharks move inland more easily with the rising water in the river. This saves them the energy they would otherwise have to expend to swim against the current of the river.

Mangroves

Mangroves are clusters of small trees that grow along riverbanks and shorelines, with their roots reaching into the water. The tangle of roots provides baby sharks with safe places to hide from hungry predators. This means that mangroves are very important shark nurseries—even for sharks that spend their adult lives at sea, such as hammerhead sharks.

Sharks on the High Seas, Sharks in the Deep Sea

From a boat, the open sea looks much the same in in all directions. But the difference from top to bottom is greater than night and day.

Sharks that swim the high seas often cover long distances and chase fish through the brightly-lit waters near the surface. But dive down... deeper... and deeper... to the twilight zone, where there is nothing left of the sun but a faint blue glow. Here you might just spot a shark with its own blue sheen. And then if you dive again, deeper still, you will find ancient sharks swimming in the dark and cold of the ocean floor.

Many sharks move between these different zones. Some swim nearer the surface at night to hunt, then dive down to darker waters during the day.

Did you know?
In the deep sea there are no plants and very few fish. The Greenland shark feeds on crab and squid as well as dead whale carcasses. These large deep-sea sharks move slowly and can live for hundreds of years.

Glow in the dark

The blackbelly lanternshark lives in the twilight zone. True to its name, it has a black belly that can glow blue in the in the dark. This may attract curious prey.

Mysterious area

The deep sea is very cold and dark, with the water pressure strong enough to crush a research vessel. This makes it very difficult to study, so scientists are just beginning to learn about it—but some kinds of sharks have been at home here for more than 200 million years.

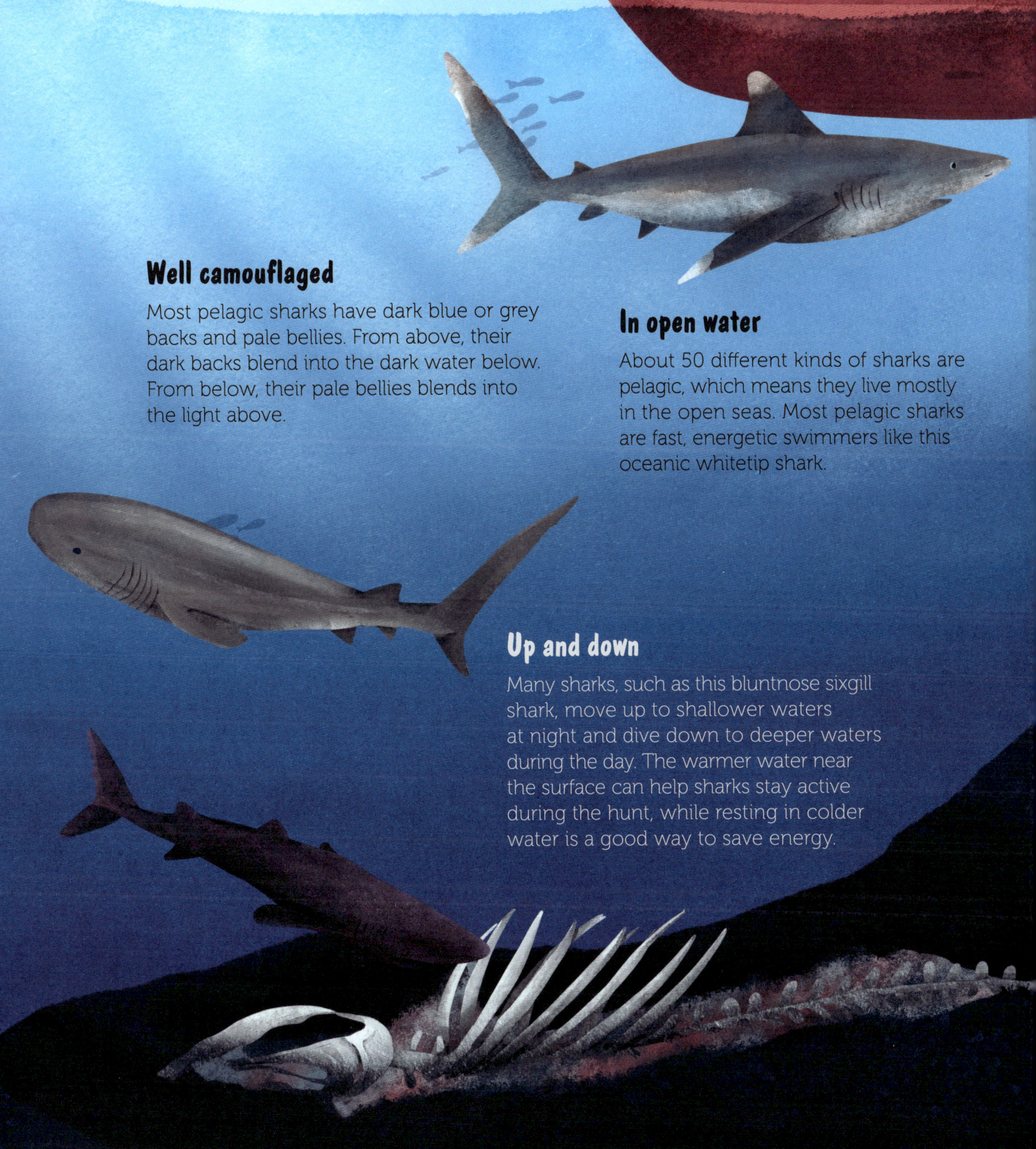

Well camouflaged

Most pelagic sharks have dark blue or grey backs and pale bellies. From above, their dark backs blend into the dark water below. From below, their pale bellies blends into the light above.

In open water

About 50 different kinds of sharks are pelagic, which means they live mostly in the open seas. Most pelagic sharks are fast, energetic swimmers like this oceanic whitetip shark.

Up and down

Many sharks, such as this bluntnose sixgill shark, move up to shallower waters at night and dive down to deeper waters during the day. The warmer water near the surface can help sharks stay active during the hunt, while resting in colder water is a good way to save energy.

Living Underwater

When you breathe in, your lungs fill with air. This gives your body the oxygen it needs. Instead of lungs, sharks use their gills to collect oxygen from the water. For this to work, sharks need to keep water flowing past their gills at all times. Different sharks have different ways of doing this.

Keep moving

Some pelagic sharks, such as mako sharks, hammerhead sharks, and white sharks, simply have to keep swimming forward with their mouths open... their whole lives. If they stop swimming, they will drown. These sharks are called ram ventilators.

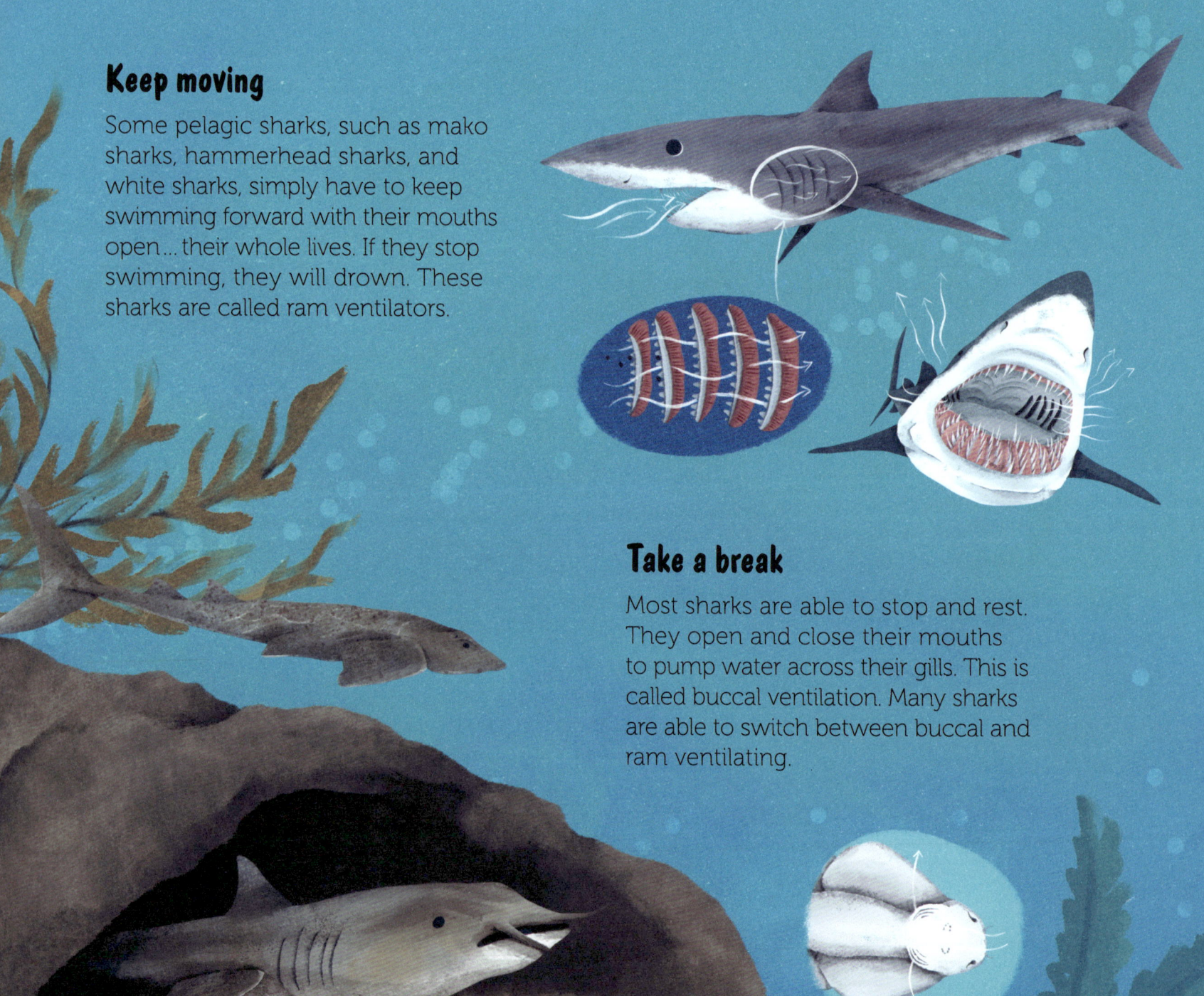

Take a break

Most sharks are able to stop and rest. They open and close their mouths to pump water across their gills. This is called buccal ventilation. Many sharks are able to switch between buccal and ram ventilating.

Do sharks pee in the sea?

Unlike people, a shark does not make watery pee to get rid of waste from its body. The sea is so salty that sharks need to retain all the water they can. Sharks can remove waste from their bodies through their skin. And yes: sharks do poop after a meal, just like you do. Shark poop comes out like a green cloud in the water.

Invisible pumping

When a tasseled wobbegong buries itself in the sand, even its mouth is covered. These types of seafloor ambush hunters pump water over their gills using openings behind their eyes called spiracles.

Great Hammerhead Shark

The great hammerhead shark is the largest of the nine species of hammerhead shark. It can live for more than 40 years and can grow to more than 16 feet (5 meters) long.

Great hammerhead sharks are ground sharks that have a wide, T-shaped head called a cephalofoil. They eat many different kinds of fish and shellfish, but their cephalofoil makes them particularly good at finding and catching rays.

This is where great hammerhead sharks have been found around the world

Great hammerhead sharks live in the shallower, warmer waters found along reefs and coastlines.

Length: 16 feet (5 meters)
Mass: 507 pounds (230 kilograms)

Eyes

With its eyes at the furthest edges of its hammer-shaped head, this shark can see above, below, forwards, and backwards all at once. The one place it can't see is directly in front of its own snout.

Mouth

The great hammerhead shark has a small, curved mouth on the underside of its body behind its cephalofoil.

Snout

The wide cephalofoil has room for many electric sensors, which allow great hammerhead sharks to scan a wide area while they hunt for rays buried in the ocean floor.

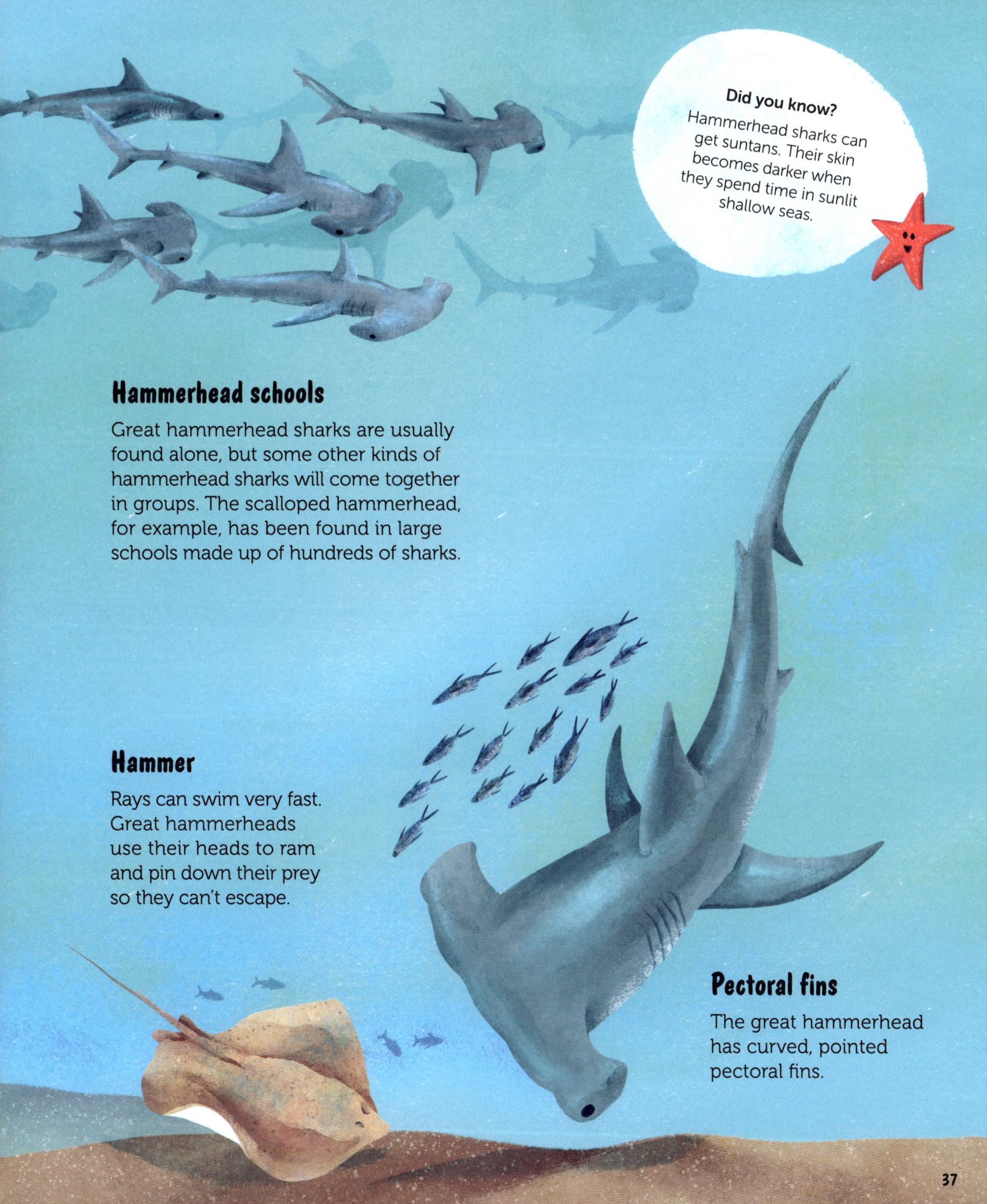

37

Did you know?
Hammerhead sharks can get suntans. Their skin becomes darker when they spend time in sunlit shallow seas.

Hammerhead schools

Great hammerhead sharks are usually found alone, but some other kinds of hammerhead sharks will come together in groups. The scalloped hammerhead, for example, has been found in large schools made up of hundreds of sharks.

Hammer

Rays can swim very fast. Great hammerheads use their heads to ram and pin down their prey so they can't escape.

Pectoral fins

The great hammerhead has curved, pointed pectoral fins.

Longnose Saw Shark

Like all saw sharks, the longnose saw shark has a long, flat, narrow snout, or rostrum, with teeth pointing out from each side. The rostrum contains many electric sensors to help the shark find small fish and shrimp along the ocean floor. A pair of long, flexible barbels midway along the rostrum help the shark feel into the sand and mud.

Length: 4 feet (1.25 meters)
Mass: 19 pounds (8.6 kilograms)

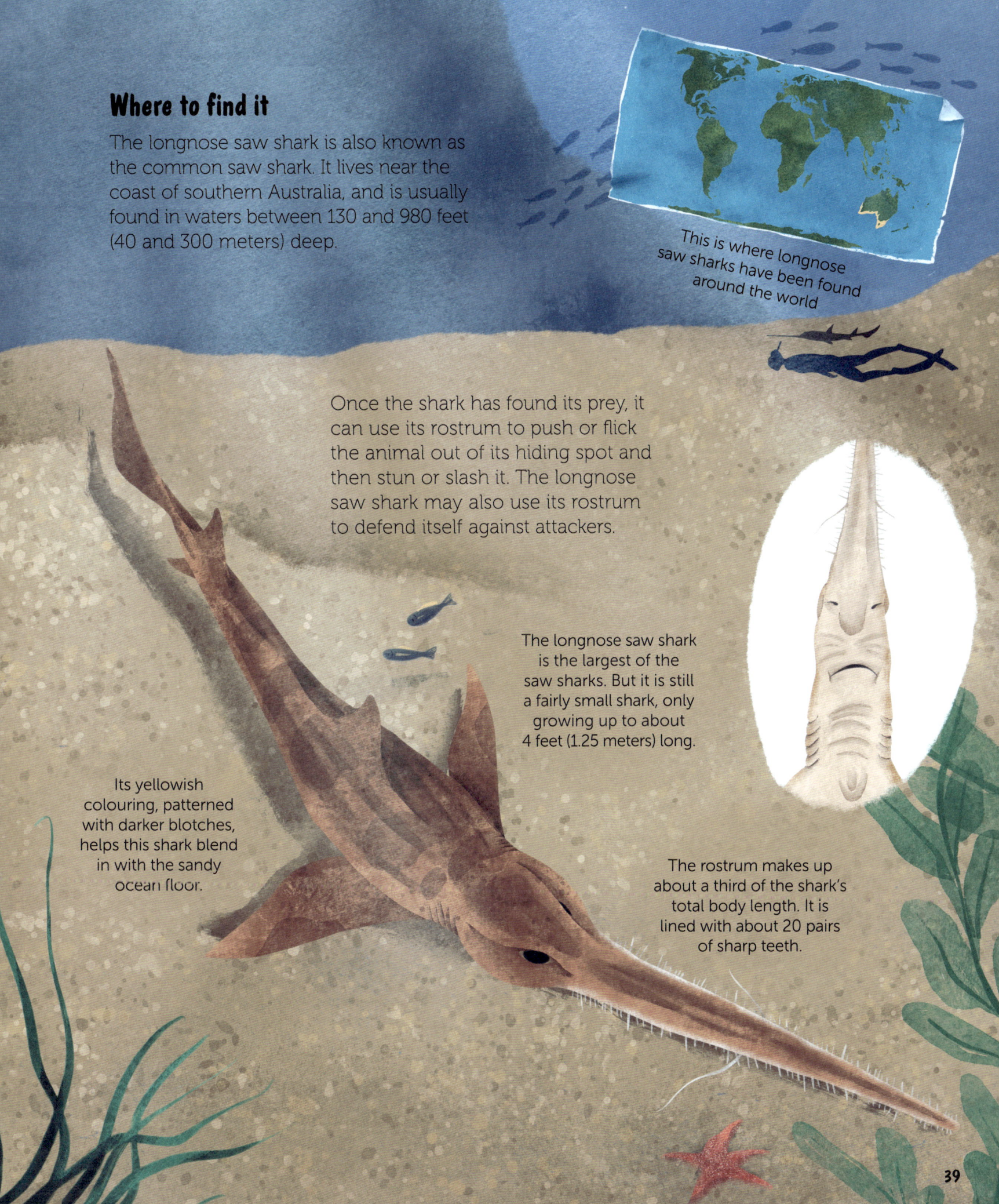

Where to find it

The longnose saw shark is also known as the common saw shark. It lives near the coast of southern Australia, and is usually found in waters between 130 and 980 feet (40 and 300 meters) deep.

This is where longnose saw sharks have been found around the world

Once the shark has found its prey, it can use its rostrum to push or flick the animal out of its hiding spot and then stun or slash it. The longnose saw shark may also use its rostrum to defend itself against attackers.

The longnose saw shark is the largest of the saw sharks. But it is still a fairly small shark, only growing up to about 4 feet (1.25 meters) long.

Its yellowish colouring, patterned with darker blotches, helps this shark blend in with the sandy ocean floor.

The rostrum makes up about a third of the shark's total body length. It is lined with about 20 pairs of sharp teeth.

Hunting Like a Shark

Each shark's hunting style is adapted to work well in its own habitat, and to help it catch its favorite foods. Over tens of millions of years, sharks have fine-tuned many different hunting strategies. Here you can catch a glimpse of a few sharks showing off their hunting skills.

The ambush

This angel shark is lying quietly on the ocean floor, covered by a layer of sand. Only its eyes peek out, keeping watch for fish swimming nearby. When a fish comes close enough... snap!

The torpedo

This great white shark has spotted a seal swimming at the surface. It dives below the seal and then swims upwards, accelerating to its top speed. The shark then rams the seal with enough force to send the seal right out of the water.

The trap

This whitetip reef shark is chasing a fish into some coral reefs. The shark's slender body allows it to follow the fish through narrow passages before trapping its prey against the sides of the reef.

The chase

This shortfin mako shark is hunting in the open ocean. It relies on its speed to chase and overtake its prey, including fast-swimming fish such as tuna.

The smack

This thresher shark is attacking a school of mackerel. It snaps its long tail in an arc that smacks over the school like a whiplash. The blow creates a shock wave in the water that stuns several of the fish, making them easy prey.

The filter

Here, a basking shark is swimming with its mouth open through water full of plankton made up of tiny plants, fish, and sea creatures. The plankton-rich water flows into the shark's open mouth and through spongy filters near its gills. The plankton is trapped in these filters for the shark to eat, while the water flows out through its gills.

The group hunt

Hundreds of spiny dogfish sharks have gathered to hunt as a group. When they spot a school of herring, they swim close together and surround the fish from all sides—including above and below. This pack-hunting strategy is what gave dogfish sharks their name.

Basking Shark

A huge mouth, a body over 28 feet (8.5 meters) long, and a tall dorsal fin that slices through the waves all make the basking shark look very fierce, but humans have nothing to fear from this mackerel shark. The basking shark is the second-largest fish in the world after the whale shark. Like its larger cousin, the basking shark is a filter feeder. It cruises slowly through the water with its mouth open, sucking in water and trapping tiny creatures in its gill rakers.

This shark is sometimes called a sailfish for the way its tall dorsal fin sticks up above the water.

This is where basking sharks have been found around the world

Mostly traveling alone

The basking shark is found in cold waters around the world. It is known for swimming across entire oceans and for taking long dives from the surface down to the deep sea. This shark is usually found alone or in pairs, but in places where there is lots of food, basking sharks may gather in large groups.

Did you know?
Baby basking sharks are the largest of all baby sharks. They are about 6.5 feet (2 meters) long at birth.

This shark mostly feeds on copepods, creatures that look like tiny shrimp.

Its five gills wrap around the top and bottom of its head on each side.

Its wide mouth and large gill rakers help trap lots of food.

Length: 28 feet (8.5 meters)
Mass: 4.3 tons (3.9 tonnes)

43

Zebra Shark

When you imagine a zebra, you probably think of its stripes first. This shark gets its name from the stripes it has on its skin when it is young. As it grows, the stripes fade away. Adult zebra sharks have pale gray or cream-colored skin patterned with dark spots.

Length: 5.6 feet (1.7 meters)
Mass: 44 pounds (20 kilograms)

Did you know?
Zebra sharks are calm and gentle. They often allow human divers to swim very close, and even to stroke them.

Particularly flexible

The zebra shark is a large carpet shark found in tropical coral reefs. It squeezes its flexible body into the narrow spaces among the reefs to hunt for crabs and small fish. Instead of biting, the zebra shark uses the muscles around its gills to suck and slurp its prey right into its mouth. It is mostly active at night. During the day, the zebra shark rests on the sea floor.

This is where zebra sharks have been found around the world

The tail of an adult zebra shark can make up half of its total body length.

Five ridges run along the length of its body—two on each side, and one down its back.

The striped pattern on a zebra shark pup makes it look a little bit like a type of poisonous sea snake. This might help protect the pup when it is small.

Its two dorsal fins are very close together. The second is smaller and flatter.

Its barbels help this shark find its prey in dark crevices.

The spots on the adult zebra shark make it look a little bit like a leopard. This can be confusing, because there is also a different kind of shark called a leopard shark (a ground shark that lives in colder waters in the North Pacific).

Shark Teeth

When people think about sharks, they often just picture mouths full of sharp teeth. In fact, each type of shark has teeth of a very particular shape and size. Its teeth are so well suited to its hunting style and preferred prey that researchers can often identify sharks from their teeth alone. Researchers can also study fossil teeth to learn about the lives of ancient sharks.

While the teeth of each kind of shark are unique, most can be grouped together into the general types you see here.

The saw

Sharks that hunt large animals, such as the great white shark, the bull shark, and the tiger shark, all have broad, triangular upper teeth. Their teeth have sharp, saw-like edges that can slice through the thick skin of large prey. The teeth in the lower jaw are narrower and are good for holding on.

The needle

Ambush hunters such as angel sharks and wobbegongs have long, needle-like teeth. These work well for quickly trapping and spearing slippery fish and squid.

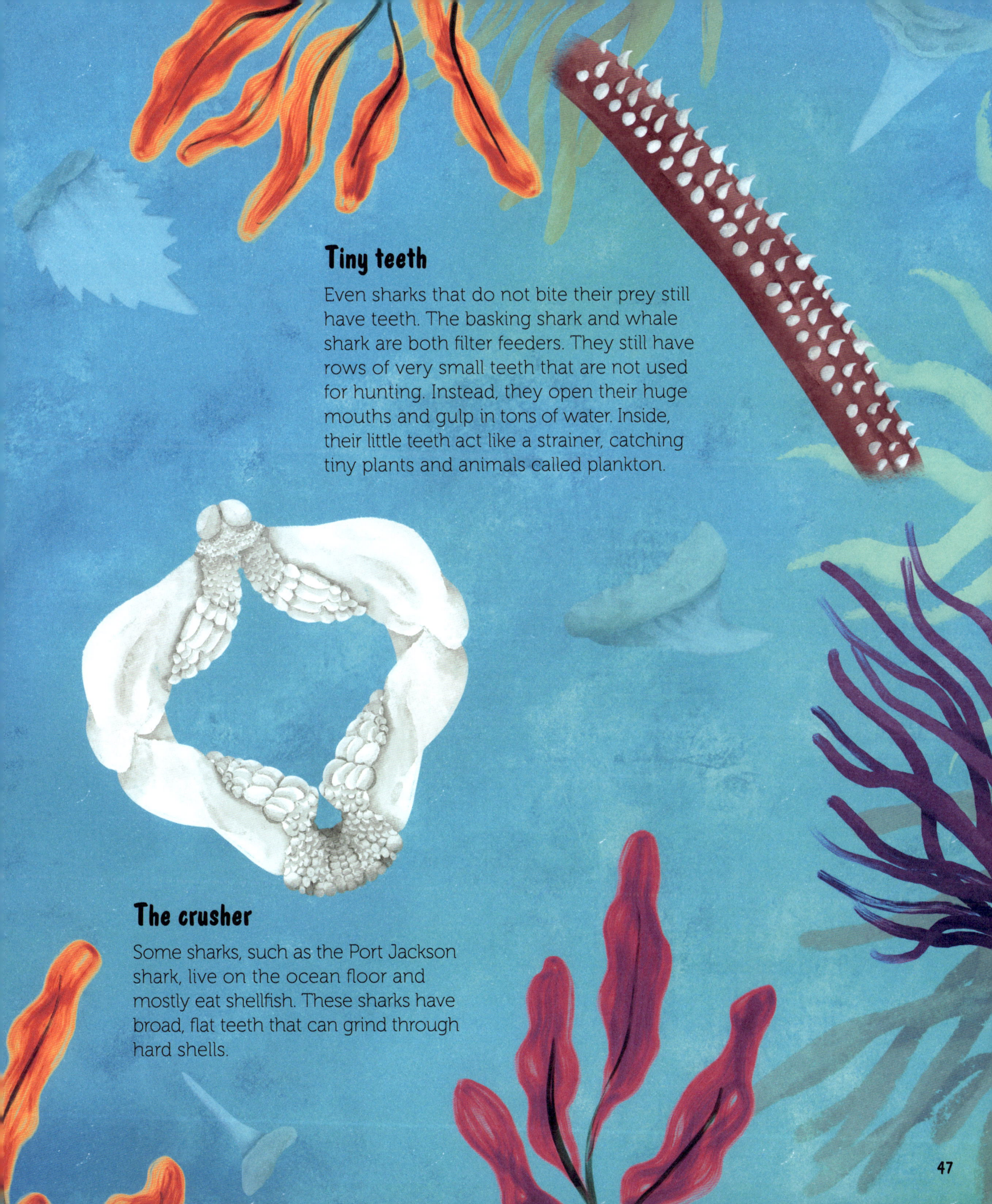

Tiny teeth

Even sharks that do not bite their prey still have teeth. The basking shark and whale shark are both filter feeders. They still have rows of very small teeth that are not used for hunting. Instead, they open their huge mouths and gulp in tons of water. Inside, their little teeth act like a strainer, catching tiny plants and animals called plankton.

The crusher

Some sharks, such as the Port Jackson shark, live on the ocean floor and mostly eat shellfish. These sharks have broad, flat teeth that can grind through hard shells.

Baby Sharks

Baby birds hatch from eggs. Baby dogs are born live from their mothers' wombs. Baby sharks can come into the world in either way—and sometimes even a bit of both. Sharks reproduce in three main ways.

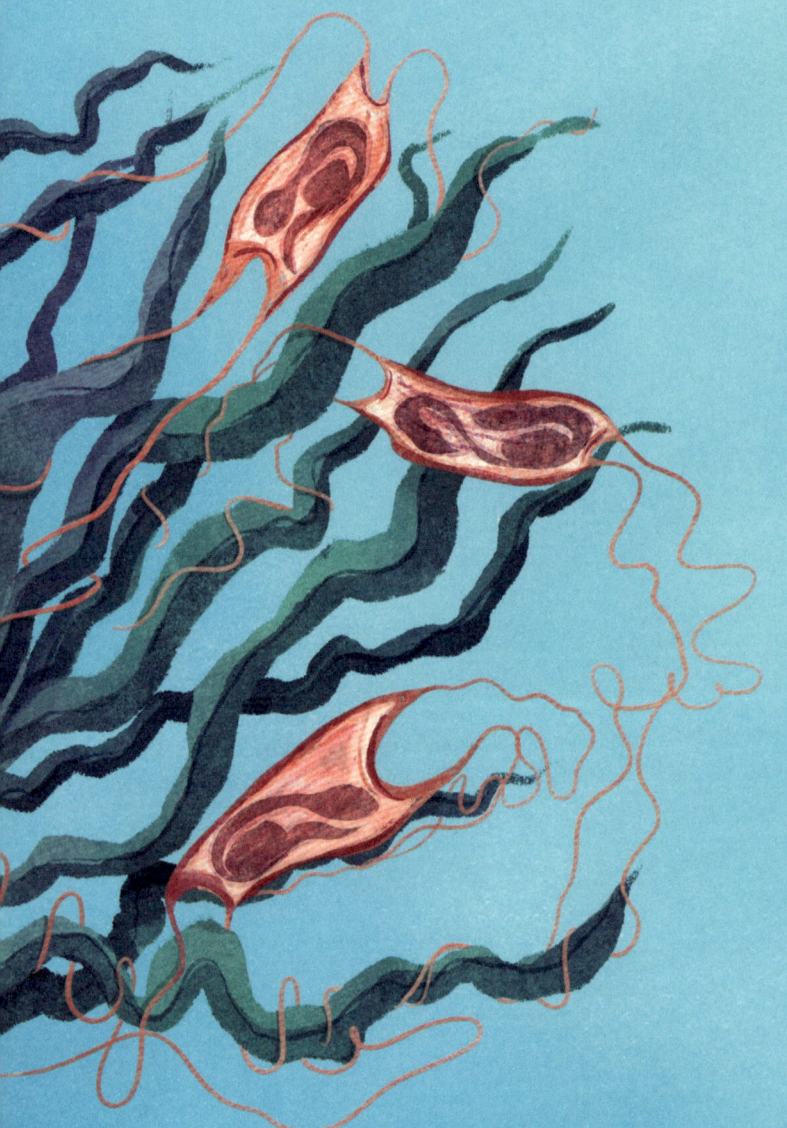

Sharks that lay eggs in the sea

Some sharks, including this brown cat shark, lay eggs. Shark eggs do not have a hard rounded shell like bird's eggs. Instead, each egg has its own tough, leathery egg case. The mother shark lays the egg case attached to seaweeds or corals so it will not be buried in the sea floor. The baby shark grows inside the egg case until it is ready to hatch. In the cold waters of the North Pacific Ocean, a baby brown cat shark will take more than two years to grow inside its egg case. It is about three inches (eight centimeters) long when it hatches.

An egg case's shape, size, and color can tell researchers what type of shark it is from. Most shark egg cases have long tendrils that help them stay attached to seaweed or coral.

The mother shark can carry many eggs at a time—but the first shark to hatch might eat the other eggs before it leaves its mother's body.

Sharks that lay eggs inside themselves

Making a shell or tough purse is one way a mother shark can protect a precious egg. Another way is to keep the egg inside herself until it is ready to hatch. As the baby grows inside its egg, it gets its food from its own egg yolk. When the egg hatches, the mother gives birth to the live baby. Great white sharks, frilled sharks, mako sharks, and thresher sharks are just some of the shark babies that are born this way.

Did you know?
A frilled shark carries its babies for more than three years before they are born.

Sharks that grow live babies

A baby shark is called a "pup," and some kinds of sharks grow their babies inside their bodies in much the same way that a puppy grows inside a mother dog. As they develop, shark pups get the food they need from their mother's body. Unlike puppies, though, shark pups leave their mother as soon as they are born. Hammerheads, bull sharks, blue sharks, and lemon sharks all give birth this way. A great hammerhead shark can give birth to more than 50 pups at a time.

Blue shark pups are born ready to hunt, but they will take many years to grow to their adult size.

Spotted Wobbegong Shark

This carpet shark looks like a living piece of ocean floor. Its flat body and patterned skin help it to blend into the sand, rocks, and corals of its home. This disguise helps the shark hide from danger and catch its food.

This is where spotted wobbegong sharks have been found around the world

The spotted wobbegong sometimes waves the very tip of its tail in a way that looks a bit like a small swimming fish. This can trick other fish into coming close.

This shark has strong pectoral fins and can use them to "walk" its body along the ocean floor or through shallow water.

The patterns of dots and circles on the shark's head make its eyes harder to spot.

The spotted wobbegong is also known as the "tasseled shark." Tassel-like fringes of skin around its head and mouth help hide the shape of its head.

Length: 6 feet (1.8 meters)
Mass: 44 pounds (20 kilograms)

Where to find it

The spotted wobbegong is found in shallow waters near the coast of Australia. During the day, it rests in caves. At night, it settles into a good hiding spot... and then waits. When creatures such as fish, crabs, and squid come near, the shark opens its jaws wide to suck them in. This shark sometimes also creeps along the ocean floor to sneak up on its prey.

Did you know?
The spotted wobbegong is a slow-moving shark that does not attack people—but watch your step! If it is touched or stepped on, this shark will bite to protect itself.

Bull Shark

The bull shark is the only shark that can move easily between salt water and fresh water. A mother bull shark will often give birth to her pups in rivers, where they are safe from other sharks. The young bull sharks will spend most of their time in fresh water. As adults, they live mostly in salt water near coastlines, swimming into bays and rivers to hunt. Very old bull sharks spend all of their time in salt water.

This is where bull sharks have been found around the world

Length: 8 feet (2.4 meters)
Mass: 639 pounds (290 kilograms)

Did you know?
Bull sharks have been found in lakes and rivers thousands of miles from the sea. They can find their way through river systems all the way to the sea and back again.

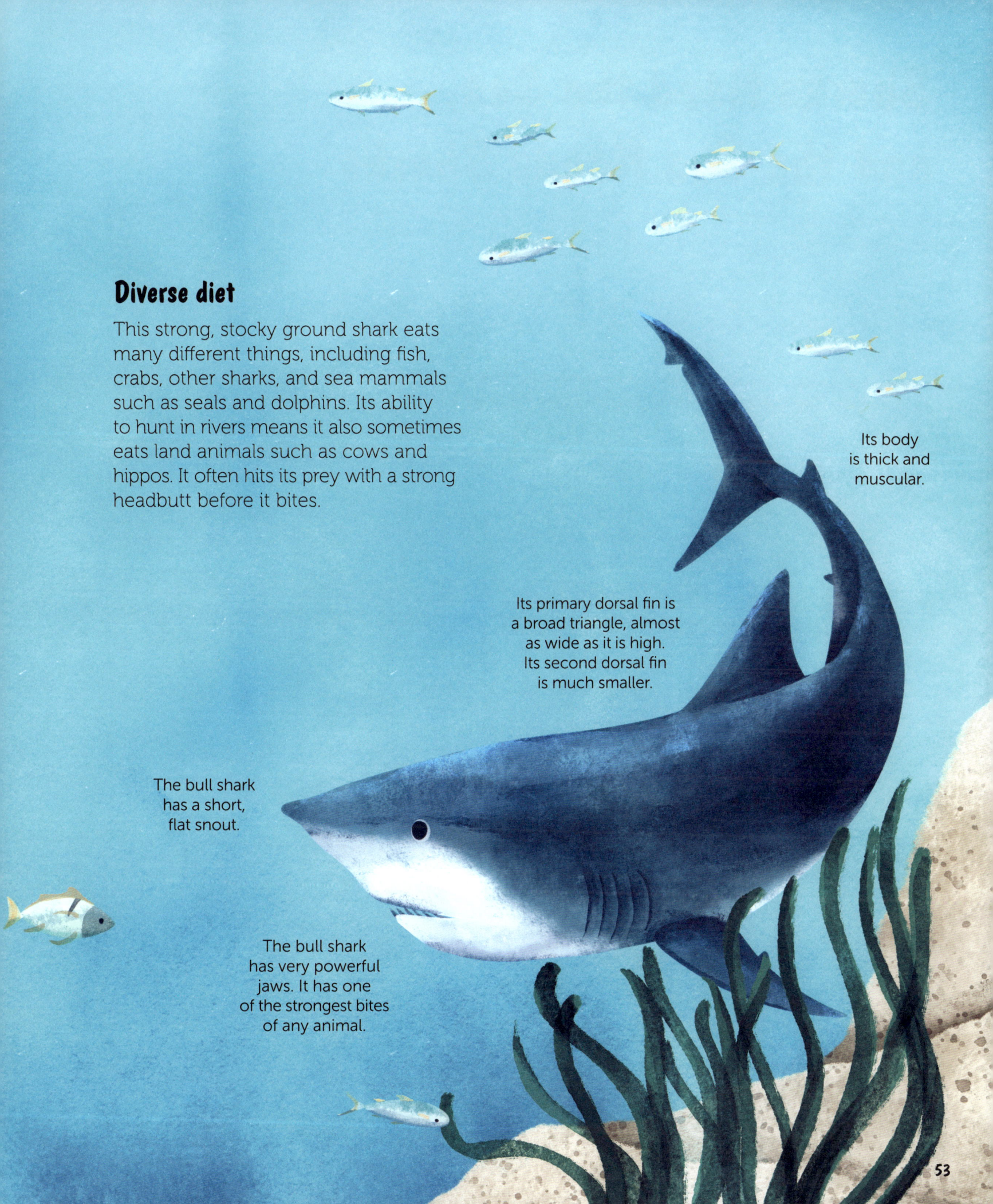

Diverse diet

This strong, stocky ground shark eats many different things, including fish, crabs, other sharks, and sea mammals such as seals and dolphins. Its ability to hunt in rivers means it also sometimes eats land animals such as cows and hippos. It often hits its prey with a strong headbutt before it bites.

Its body is thick and muscular.

Its primary dorsal fin is a broad triangle, almost as wide as it is high. Its second dorsal fin is much smaller.

The bull shark has a short, flat snout.

The bull shark has very powerful jaws. It has one of the strongest bites of any animal.

Sharks Need the Sea, and the Sea Needs Sharks

To survive, sharks need healthy seas full of fish. And to stay healthy and full of fish, seas need sharks.

Sharks are not the only creatures that need healthy seas. So does every plant, animal, and person on Earth. More than half of the oxygen we breathe comes from the sea, and the sea provides food and water for the whole planet. This means that taking care of the seas is very important. One of the best ways to do this is to make sure there are plenty of sharks. Here you can see just a few of the ways that sharks help keep the sea healthy.

In most of the places they live, sharks are the top predators. Here, fish are grazing on the sea grass meadows below. If there are too many fish, they will eat up all the plants. Sharks help keep the number of fish in balance so the meadows can regenerate.

Sharks have a better chance of catching slower, sick, or injured fish. By eating the weaker fish, sharks help keep the rest of the fish population strong and healthy.

Shark poop fuels reef growth

Some species of shark swim out into the open ocean at night to hunt and eat and then return to the reef during the day, where they rest... and poop. Their poop provides the reefs and sea meadows with nutrients that help them grow.

Researchers can often tell whether an area of ocean is healthy just by the number of sharks they find there. If the area is home to sharks, that means it is home to many other fish and plants as well.

Sharks can help even when they don't catch fish. When sharks are nearby, fish will stop grazing to hide or swim away. Keeping fish moving is another way sharks help make sure the meadows have time to grow.

Goblin Shark

The goblin shark is a mackerel shark that spends most of its time in the cold, dark waters of the deep sea. It is slow and sluggish until it is ready to attack, and then it flicks a switch and transforms to full-on action mode. It opens its mouth, shoots its jaws forward, and snaps them shut around its prey—all in less than one-third of a second. This jaw motion is called slingshot feeding.

This is where goblin sharks have been found around the world

0 seconds

Its jaws are usually tucked neatly into its head.

This shark's body is soft and not very muscular. It is not a strong swimmer.

Its long, soft snout is packed with electric sensors that help it find prey in the ocean's dark depths.

0.15 seconds

Length: 11.5 feet (3.5 meters)
Mass: 387 pounds (180 kilograms)

0.2 seconds

0.28 seconds

The goblin shark is pale at birth and becomes a darker grayish-pink as it gets older. The pink colour comes from blood vessels beneath the skin.

Frilled Shark

During the day, this eel-like shark rests near the ocean floor, up to 5,000 feet (1,500 meters) under water. At night, it swims up to the surface to hunt fish, smaller sharks, and squid. Its slender body can expand to swallow these animals whole. The frilled shark sometimes curls its tail against a rock and then pushes off to shoot quickly through the water.

This is where frilled sharks have been found around the world

Did you know?
Both the goblin shark and frilled shark are sometimes called "living fossils." They each belong to very ancient shark families.

The frilled shark has six gill slits, each with an uneven frilly edge. The first pair of gills meets under the jaw like a ruffled collar.

Its dorsal fin is small and set far back on its body.

The frilled shark is also called the "lizard shark" because its flattened snout and narrow nostrils make its head look like that of a lizard or snake.

Its pectoral fins are very small and rounded.

Tiger Shark

The tiger shark is a large ground shark found in warm coastal waters all around the world. The skin of baby tiger sharks is gray and marked with darker spots and blotches. As the babies grow, they develop the stripes that give this shark its name. The stripes fade again as the adult shark becomes older.

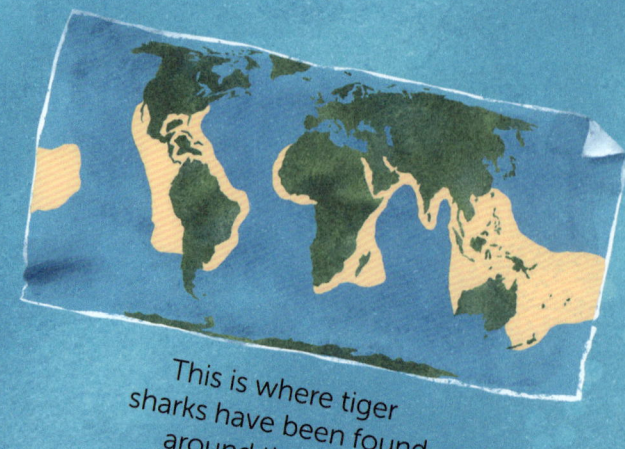

This is where tiger sharks have been found around the world

Did you know?

Young tiger sharks spend most of their time in bays and other sheltered waters. This may help them hide from the adult tiger sharks that might eat them.

Length: 13 feet (4 meters)
Mass: 1,400 pounds (635 kilograms)

Ocean-sized appetite

The tiger shark is known for its big appetite.
It hunts alone at night and eats many different
things, including fish, other sharks, sea turtles,
dolphins, seals, sea birds, squid, and shellfish,
as well as the bodies of dead whales and
sharks. It even eats garbage such as plastic
bags, wooden signs, old tires, and tin cans.

Its snout
is short and
rounded.

The tiger shark is the
fourth largest of all the
sharks, after the whale
shark, basking shark,
and great white shark.

Its mouth is wide
with large,
saw-edged teeth.

Its back and sides
are medium
to dark gray, and
its belly is pale gray
or yellow-gray.

Angel Shark

The angel shark is one type of shark in the broader angel shark family. Different kinds of angel sharks live in different parts of the world, but they are all found in warm, shallow waters living on the ocean floor. With their flat bodies and wide, wing-like pectoral fins, angel sharks are often confused with rays.

Length: 6 feet (1.8 meters)
Mass: 110 pounds (50 kilograms)

The bottom lobe of its tail is larger than the top lobe. This helps the shark quickly lift off the sea floor to catch its prey.

Its pectoral fin is separate from its head, while a ray's pectoral fin is fused to its head.

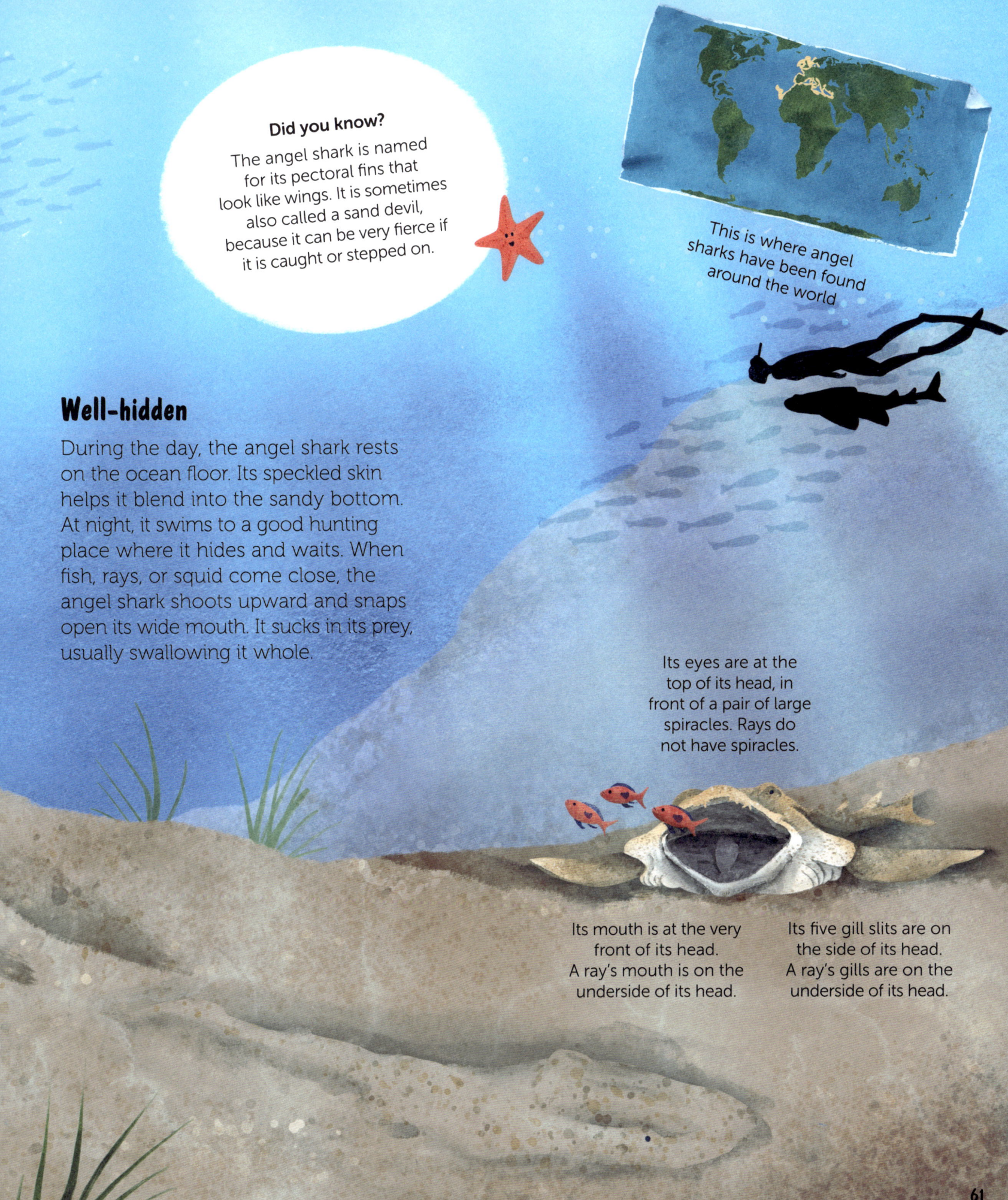

Did you know?

The angel shark is named for its pectoral fins that look like wings. It is sometimes also called a sand devil, because it can be very fierce if it is caught or stepped on.

This is where angel sharks have been found around the world

Well-hidden

During the day, the angel shark rests on the ocean floor. Its speckled skin helps it blend into the sandy bottom. At night, it swims to a good hunting place where it hides and waits. When fish, rays, or squid come close, the angel shark shoots upward and snaps open its wide mouth. It sucks in its prey, usually swallowing it whole.

Its eyes are at the top of its head, in front of a pair of large spiracles. Rays do not have spiracles.

Its mouth is at the very front of its head. A ray's mouth is on the underside of its head.

Its five gill slits are on the side of its head. A ray's gills are on the underside of its head.

Sharks and People

Sharks are strong, wild animals and skilled hunters. They can be ferocious if they feel that they are in danger. They are also curious, and may explore what things are by biting them. This all means that sharks can be dangerous to people. It is important to be careful in areas where sharks live. A few dozen people around the world are killed by sharks each year.

And every year, tens of millions of sharks are killed by people. Millions of sharks are caught for their meat and fins. Millions more are killed by nets set to catch other kinds of fish. As people build big cities, ports, and platforms along coastlines and on the sea floor, sharks are running of places to live. Pollution makes it harder for sharks to survive and have healthy pups.

The good news is that many people are now working hard to save sharks. These pages show just some of the ways people can help.

Scientists can sometimes gather eggs from sharks that live in aquariums, and then raise the shark pups until they are big enough to have a good chance of surviving in the wild. The scientists then release them into areas they would live in naturally.

One of the most important things people can do is protect areas of the sea where sharks and other ocean animals can safely live, grow, and have lots of babies. These protected areas help keep the ocean healthy and give sharks a better chance of survival.

Scientists and fishers are working together to design better nets and other fishing gear so that fewer sharks are accidentally caught each year.

What you can do

You can help sharks by learning more about them and sharing what you know. The more people know and care about these amazing animals, the more will be done to protect them. And when you help protect sharks, you help protect all the creatures in the sea.

Studying Sharks

It is not easy to study animals that spend all their time under water. People can sometimes swim with sharks to watch how they go about their lives—but only for short periods, and only in shallow seas. Researchers use many different tools to help them learn more. Even so, very little is known about many shark species. This is especially true for sharks that live in the deep ocean. This means that there is lots of interesting work ahead.

Tonic immobility

If you turn a shark onto its back, it will go still and quiet. This is called tonic immobility. It does not hurt the shark. Researchers can turn a shark onto its back to measure or tag it and then gently turn it upright again to let it go unharmed.

Tracking sharks

Researchers can attach tags to the backs of larger sharks that send tracking signals to satellites. This lets researchers see how far the shark travels and where it goes. Because many sharks travel across entire oceans, researchers from different countries like to work together to share what they are learning.

Examining sharks

Researchers can study dead sharks
to learn about their age, size, and
weight. Bite marks and other scars
on the shark's skin can tell stories
about the shark's life. Researchers can
also look inside the shark's stomach
to see what it has been eating.

Sharks in aquariums

Some kinds of sharks, especially smaller
sharks, are able to live in aquariums.
This gives researchers a better chance to
study them up close. Still, it is hard to know
whether sharks in tanks are behaving in
the same ways as they would in the wild.

Glossary

Ampullae of Lorenzini: A sense organ that allows a shark to detect nearby electric charges.

Anal fin: A single small stabilizing fin pointing down from the belly of the shark near its tail. Not all sharks have an anal fin.

Angel shark: One of the eight main groups of sharks found today. Angel sharks have broad, flat bodies.

Barbels: Whisker-like sensory organs found on the head of some sharks that can help the shark find prey buried in sand or mud.

Breach: The action of leaping clear of the water. Some sharks, such as the great white and shortfin mako, are known for breaching. Many marine mammals such as dolphins and some whales also breach.

Buccal ventilation: Absorbing oxygen by pumping water across the gills. Sharks that use buccal ventilation can continue to take in oxygen while at rest.

Bullhead shark: One of the eight main groups of sharks found today. They get their name from hornlike bumps on their heads.

Cartilage: The tough, bendable stuff that makes up your ears and the tip of your nose. Cartilage is lighter and more flexible than bone.

Cartilaginous fish: A family of fish with skeletons made of cartilage instead of bone. Sharks, rays, and chimaera are examples of cartilaginous fish.

Carpet shark: One of the eight main groups of sharks found today. Carpet sharks are found mostly near the ocean floor in shallow seas.

Caudal fin: The tail fin of the shark, divided into an upper lobe and a lower lobe. The caudal fin propels the shark through the water.

Cephalofoil: The broad, T-shaped head of a hammerhead shark.

Copepods: Tiny shrimp-like creatures that can be found in large clusters in oceans all around the world. Copepods are a main food item for filter-feeding sharks and whales.

Dogfish shark: One of the eight main groups of sharks found today. Dogfish sharks have two dorsal fins, one of which may have a sharp, poisonous spine.

Dorsal fin: A single stabilizing fin that points up from the top of the shark's back. All sharks have at least one dorsal fin, and some have two.

Dorsal side: The back of the shark.

Fork length: The length of the shark from the tip of its snout to the nearest point in the fork of its tail. Fork length can be used to compare the size of different types of sharks with different tail shapes.

Gills: The organs behind the head through which sharks take in oxygen. Most sharks have five pairs of gills, though some have six or seven.

Gill rakers: Small comb-like structures located on the gills of some filter-feeding sharks. The rakers trap food that is carried in the water flowing past the gills.

Ground shark: One of the eight main groups of sharks found today. This group includes hammerhead sharks and blue sharks.

Keel: A marine term for a long, narrow ridge. Some sharks, such as the whale shark, have ridges known as keels running the length of their bodies.

Lateral line: A sense organ that allows fish, including sharks, to detect movement in the water. The lateral line runs the length of the body of most fish.

Mackerel shark: One of the eight main groups of sharks found today. This group includes some of the best-known sharks, such as the great white shark.

Mangroves: Coastal habitats made up of clusters of small trees and shrubs that grow along riverbanks and shorelines with their roots reaching into the water.

Megalodon: Possibly the largest of the prehistoric sharks. This huge hunter lived between 3 million and 23 million years ago.

Nares: Another word for nostrils. A shark does not breathe through its nares, instead using them for its powerful sense of smell.

Pectoral fins: The front pair of fins that point to each side. These are used for steering and maneuvering.

Pelagic: Living mostly or entirely in the open ocean.

Pelvic fins: A shark's hind pair of fins that point to each side. These are used for steering and maneuvering.

Plankton: A general term for the collections of tiny plants and animals that drift through the oceans all around the world.

Ram ventilation: Absorbing oxygen by actively moving the gills through the water. Sharks that rely on ram ventilation must keep swimming forward to take in oxygen.

Sawfish shark: One of the eight main groups of sharks found today. Sawfish sharks have long, toothy snouts that look like saws.

Sixgill shark: One of the eight main groups of sharks found today. Sharks in this group have six or seven pairs of gill slits, and only one dorsal fin.

Slingshot feeding: A feeding motion in which the jaws shoot forward from the underside of the head, snap shut around prey, and then retract. Several types of shark are slingshot feeders.

Spiracle: An opening behind the eye that allows a shark to pump water across its gills.

Spyhopping: The action of raising the head out of the water to look around. Some sharks, including the great white shark, are known to spyhop. Many marine mammals such as whales, seals, and sea lions also spyhop.

Total length: The length of the shark from the tip of its snout to the furthest tip of its tail. Total length can be used to compare the size of two sharks of the same type.

Tonic immobility: A conscious but quiet state that many sharks enter if they are turned onto their backs.

Twilight zone: The area of the ocean at a depth just beyond the reach of sunlight, where the water is lit only by a faint blue glow.

Ventral side: The belly of the shark.

Darcy Dobell *Dedicated to all those working to protect and rebuild healthy seas, with my utmost admiration and gratitude.*

Becky Thorns *For Timothy, I hope you love sharks as much when you're older as you do right now.*

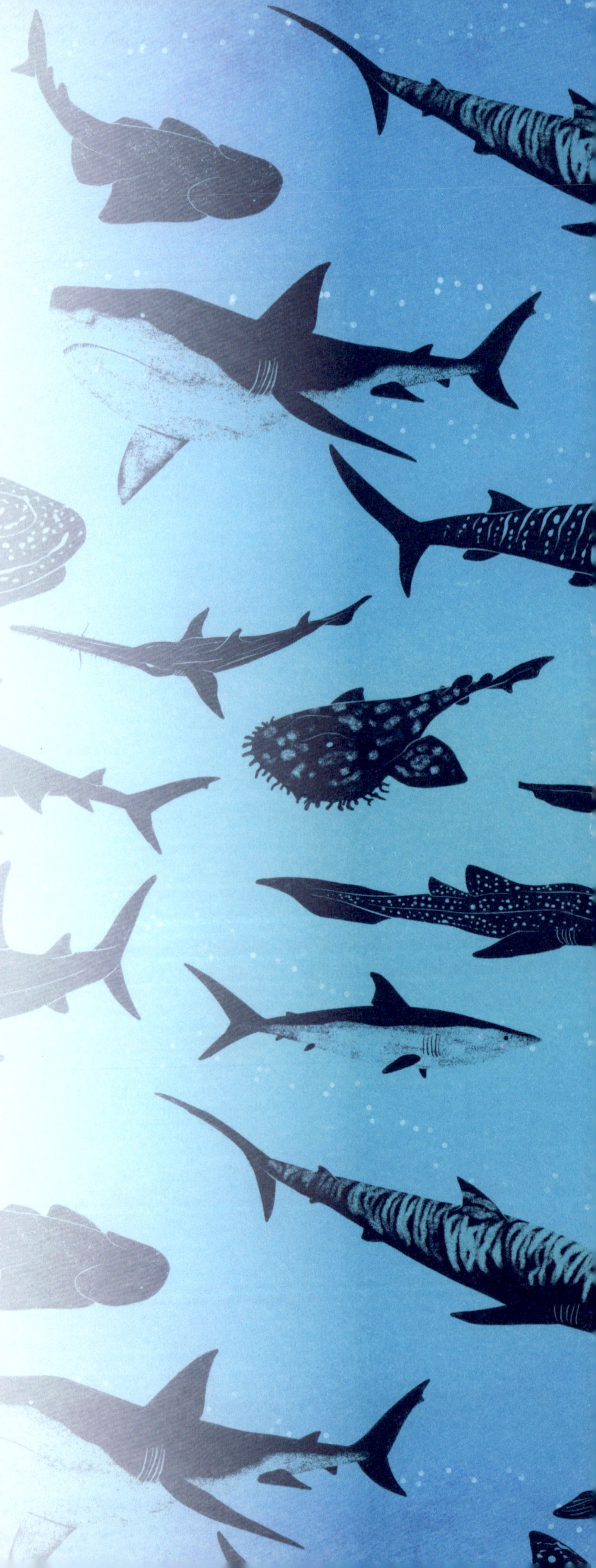

The World of Sharks
Get to Know the Fascinating Creatures of the Oceans

Illustrated by Becky Thorns
Written by Darcy Dobell

This book was conceived, edited, and designed by Little Gestalten

Edited by Robert Klanten and Friederike Christoph

Fact-checking by Darcy Dobell

Design and layout by Melanie Ullrich
Typefaces: Polka MN by Mecanorma, Museo by Jos Buivenga

Printed by Grafisches Centrum Cuno GmbH&Co.KG, Calbe (Saale)
Made in Germany

Published by Little Gestalten, Berlin 2025
ISBN 978-3-96704-780-6

1st Edition, 2025

For more information, and to order books, please visit
www.gestalten.com/collections/little-gestalten

Die Gestalten Verlag GmbH & Co. KG
Mariannenstrasse 9–10
10999 Berlin, Germany
hello@gestalten.com

Bibliographic information published by the Deutsche Nationalbibliothek.
The Deutsche Nationalbibliothek lists this publication in the Deutsche Nationalbibliografie; detailed bibliographic data are available online at www.dnb.de.

This book was printed on paper certified according to the standards of the FSC®.